# How to Draw Fire

Poems

*by*

# Marcus Whalbring

*Finishing Line Press*
Georgetown, Kentucky

# How to Draw Fire

Poems

Copyright © 2020 by Marcus Whalbring
ISBN 978-1-64662-135-4 First Edition
All rights reserved under International and Pan-American Copyright Conventions. No part of this book may be reproduced in any manner whatsoever without written permission from the publisher, except in the case of brief quotations embodied in critical articles and reviews.

## ACKNOWLEDGMENTS

Thank you to the Editors of the following publications:

"Before Cursing God, I Pray to My Wife" appeared in *Spry Literary Journal*
"We Must Go" and "Sunflower" Appeared in *Underwood Press*

Thank you to Hoa Nguyen and Laura Van Prooyen for your guidance and support with this book.

Thank you Emily, for every single day and every single thing. I love you.

Publisher: Leah Maines
Editor: Christen Kincaid
Cover Art: Marcus Whalbring
Author Photo: Emily Whalbring
Cover Design: Marcus Whalbring

Printed in the USA on acid-free paper.
Order online: www.finishinglinepress.com
　　　　　　also available on amazon.com

Author inquiries and mail orders:
Finishing Line Press
P. O. Box 1626
Georgetown, Kentucky 40324
U. S. A.

# Table of Contents

**I.**
Sunday Mornings ........................................................................ 1
Walking to School ...................................................................... 2
Riding in the Backseat ............................................................... 3
Impression .................................................................................. 4
Before I Left Grandma's House ................................................. 5
Star Lab ....................................................................................... 6
My Childhood Taught Me ......................................................... 7
Sunflower .................................................................................... 9

**II.**
Sandman ................................................................................... 13
My Dad Called to Ask Why .................................................... 14
To My Father's Surgical Incision Healing .............................. 15
The Outfielders ........................................................................ 16
At the Golf Course Afterhours ............................................... 18
To Franz Wright ....................................................................... 19
Hump Day ................................................................................ 21
Sneeze ....................................................................................... 22
To the Shroud of Turin ........................................................... 23
Taxonomy ................................................................................. 25
Out of Order ............................................................................. 27

**III.**
Thumb War .............................................................................. 31
Love Poem ................................................................................ 32
I'm in the Attic: a Dream-Memory ........................................ 33
Before Cursing God, I Pray to My Wife ................................ 34
A Pond Walk ............................................................................ 36
A Bridge of Paper .................................................................... 37
Diagnosis .................................................................................. 38
Imagining Us in a Jewelry Commercial ................................ 40
We Must Go ............................................................................. 42
My Children Sleeping ............................................................. 43
In the Gray Yard ...................................................................... 44
Walking on the Beach with My Son ...................................... 46
Lost ........................................................................................... 47
Most People Think the Sky ..................................................... 49

Grandma's Kitchen ........................................................................ 50
Remembering How She Died ...................................................... 52

## IV.
A Box............................................................................................ 57
The Balloon .................................................................................. 60
Hotel Room .................................................................................. 61
I'm Still Finding Dead Marigolds................................................ 62
Rain ............................................................................................... 63
Eggs ............................................................................................... 64
High Light .................................................................................... 65
How to Draw Fire........................................................................ 67
Afterlife......................................................................................... 68

# I.

## Sunday Mornings

My older brother and I climbed headstones
while adults talked and shuffled from pews.

They laughed off details of local news
while we pulled each other up on ledges

nearly collapsing under our delicate bones.
We played hide-and-seek, rode atop them

like they were skeletal horses
before we hurried downhill

to where the oldest lay green
with moss slowly erasing their names.

Maybe their living families would shame us
but we were too alive to worry. Maybe time

held us captive, made us two moths
stuffed in a pocketful of other moths slowly eating itself.

Maybe, but we laughed busy
in a garden that, in the wind, sounded

like the hush hovering over unfallen rain.
Like the rain, we looked for each other

in a game we'd invented and loved
so much we'd forgotten to give it a name.

## Walking to School

One of those cooler mornings in October
I see myself nine-years-old,
this boy who doesn't think yet about

one leaf's loneliness as it falls, only
their laughter and his as he kicks through
their empty pages crowding the sidewalk.

He smiles back at ghosts
taped to a neighbor's windows. Their repose
reminds him not of shrouds but cartoons.

Now as I follow him down
that familiar sidewalk
I am a ghost haunting him.

See him carelessly caress leaves
still holding the short branches
as he walks under them.

See him yawn without complaint, stop
at the curb until the crossing guard guides him
to the other side. And I sigh

so close to the boy's ear, he turns
and looks through me without smiling
then turns back and crosses the street.

# Riding in the Backseat

I remember the woods. I squinted
through the dark as far as I could.
Winter. Our tires splashed through slush.

My parents talked in the front
about their plans, which would never come
to pass. Maybe we should move? Maybe
in late spring when the weather is warmer
we'll think about it more. The heater hummed.

Should we take a trip this summer?
Yes. Where? Somewhere new, far from here.
Their voices shook casually through patches
of rocks in the road grinding against the wheels.

Occasionally a pothole's pound made them jump
then laugh. Oh well. I watched the woods
thinking how scared, how lonely one would feel
out there. In thirty minutes or so we'd be safe

at home. I yawned knowing we wouldn't get lost.
Mom turned back to check on me.
Are you sleeping Marcus? Almost.

# Impression

I would not wait for him to look away
before stepping on the wet cement again.
My stepdad had smoothed it an hour
before, and written my and my brother's names
with a nail in a corner by the porch steps
above the year: 1990. The first time,
the sole of my size Youth 1 shoe
almost rested on the surface. "Get
your foot off!" he called from the window
and I retreated a step, then stared longer
into the glisten and the dark its wet brought out,
which separated it from the pale, cracked
concrete of the older sidewalks.

And because I had to know, my shoe
intruded again the surface I felt soften and sink.
He saw. And the air required to voice his anger
could have dried it instantly. Instead
I fell back to the grass
where I stayed. That wrong step shows now
where I was that day, so random in position
the thousands of passersby who see it,
to this day, must pause their thoughts
and conversations long enough to look down,
then up into the safe softness of the clouds
and wonder why.

# Before I Left Grandma's House

My right hand glutted with rocks
at the roadside, I waited for the right car.
Many times, I'd imagined
pelting one with gravel as it passed,
but I was too scared to attack
anything more than the ghost of a car,
rocks rattling like chains on the pavement.
I haunted that road every day, pretending.
I wasn't pretending anymore.

The blood in my hands warmed the rocks
like an engine above my head
when a wood-paneled station wagon screwed
around the turn. I paused. And followed
through, letting go the rocks
that shattered the roof,
a thousand angry grandmas
tapping a fingernail
on the same glass table. The car stopped.
She stepped out. My mouth dropped.
She unsheathed her finger
and threatened, "Don't you ever again…"

The glory of the moment hardened
in my head like granite. We stood
alone in that road lost. I'd released
her from life's considerations.
Then she released us both after she
walked back to her car, rattled,
tripping on rocks, driving
into my memory,
less than a stone's throw
from my imagination.

## Star Lab

We sat in a circle. Our teacher
thumbed a switch up, unwinding
night's threads, yarns of light

writing shapes the color of heat.
A queen, she said, suffered a seat
sometimes upside down—she had to

for her daughter. And the water carrier
Zeus drew up from the fields
to serve thirsty gods.

How could the world not feel
smaller than that room,
that room we filled with our leaving,

letting in the daylight
and its boring, unstoried swelter?
"Quiet in the hall," she said.

We sat in our chairs
and finished adding fractions,
the tips of our pencils pointing

down as they swirled
and stopped, and whispered,
swirled, and stopped.

# My Childhood Taught Me

To turn a porch swing into a submarine console.
To bobsled down the sidewalk in a Radioflyer
using Mom's crabapple tree as finish line.

To gather rain from the crest of a slide with my sleeve.
The rhythm in Mom's voice,
how it stumbled my name when she found
Superman's plastic head in the VCR.

And the cracks in the pavement
veining the path between home and school.
Then the drums, to feel them
with my throat before I heard them
drive the pulsing Independence Day Parade.

And nights of winter stillness,
the patience of spring.
The last day of school, roaming
room to room with so much nothing
to do. To use the cool side of the pillow
on warm nights, and the warm side of toast,
on cool mornings, where butter melts best.

Gravel's growl when feet stop without slowing.
Summer's pace, like paper-thin curtains
by an open window. Staying up
in a layer of blue light, late
watching shows our parents called off-limits. Late
mornings still too early for a slice of lemon cake.
To break a branch off a hill as I passed
without knowing why. Decay
my teeth all summer, sleeping in.

And to find a dead bird in the back yard
and bury it behind the garage
in a shoe box with a flower I'd made of paper
at school that day. To pin a pillowcase

around my neck and fly from the top bunk.

To fall a choir of pebbles into Gas Creek
where I'd sit for hours on a concrete bridge.
When she cried alone in her room, to try
to be the absence of winter in Mom's life.
To rest alone on a hillside
that overlooks the worst river in the world
on the worst day of the worst week
anyone could have at camp. To feel
how brown that river sleeps
against the inside of my head when I *can't* sleep.

To see the ocean the first time
and drift like a flag in its froth.
To see Chicago from a hotel room,
smell the deep chlorine of the indoor pool,
behold glasses wrapped in paper, pay-per-view, the view
thirty flights up of storm light and city traffic.

How long to stand on frozen puddles
before the ice breaks. How long
a crayon stays solid in a microwave.
The creaking snow under a sled slowing
where a hill straightens
at the start of winter break. To form,
from the same snow, tunnels in a drift,
to crawl in and hide until sundown.

To make—that is, to fashion—from fragments
of dead fireflies new earrings for a neighbor girl
in winter's absence. To know she wore them home
because she glowed
through every dark yard along the way.

# Sunflower

The biggest I've seen—
the size of a steering wheel
in some friend's grandma's garden—drove
the world into me,

dragging the sun with it,
reached like a voice from a cave
where it's always night, knocked
me down without touching me, then turned

away. That night Mom had to lie
with me until I fell asleep,
tell me I'd be alright
and the next morning

I watched some cartoon I loved
and ate a sugared cereal,
a stem of sunlight resting
on the edge of my bowl.

## II.

# Sandman

Enter your father shirtless in the driveway
as if from antiquity or a dream
raking gravel with his sneakers
while Metallica rattles the garage windows
*Say your prayers, little one.*
*Don't forget, my son,*
*to include everyone,*
he sings to himself and into his beer bottle
between free-throws. His knees

won't let him jump enough after shots falling
short, but he shuffles himself after them
because his doctor says, *Something's wrong,*
*shut the light, heavy thoughts tonight*,
he needs to keep his heart moving
among other directives keeping him alive,
no more drinking or smoking,
more rice and vegetables,
get plenty of *sleep with one eye open,*
*gripping your pillow tight,*
get screened, and know your numbers:
cholesterol and blood pressure, sugar.

Weeds pierce the gravel. Vines vein
like fissures down the fence
he built the year you moved in
when he hung the goal too
where it rusts without breaking now. Now
he stands plastered with sweat, his bones
cracking like fallen statues. His knees
dissolving like statues fallen but not shattered
yet, until they grind to grain, to earth
to become earth
again, like fences, like goals, like shots
taken that never land, *never-never land*
*take my hand*
*We're off to never-never land*
*take my hand.*

## My Dad Called to Ask Why

We don't talk. I
don't know. *I don't know.*
I stared at the tree
out the window.
*Could you lower your voice?*
and every dead leaf silently
falling was *sorry,*
*sorry, sorry…*

*We'll fix this*, he said, and I
nodded, which he couldn't hear,
so I said, *Yes* and *sorry.*

*Let's do something*
*together,* he said and asked
*What do you like to do?* and I said
*I don't like to do anything*
and he laughed and
I laughed
a little.

The call ended
with a promise to meet
at his house where he'd
grill chicken or steak
Friday evening. Yes.
To call each other once a week. Yes.
Until we fix this, this
silent streak.

*Was that your dad?*
my wife had to ask
a second time because still
I stared out the window
not listening,
so I said, *Yes* and *sorry.*

# To My Father's Surgical Incision Healing

1
Expensive bruise in the shape of a cocoon,
black of an open mouth
and blue of a closed bridge over grey water,
you live an inch long because
he lived, we thought, an inch from dying.

2
As a kid I heard his heart too,
every other weekend, how it boiled black coffee
and beef grease and nicotine,
my ear warming, like you, against him.
Always against him.

3
How many like you, on the skin of a sun,
keep alive its fire? I've tried to find
the way deeper, the middle of his night. Yes,
you're a mouth more closed than a cocoon
but my ear still burns to hear you.

## The Outfielders

When we questioned it, they said, *You're out
there because you have a good arm.*
But we had to wonder. The coaches' kids
or the coaches' friends' kids
at the pitcher's mound, first base, shortstop,
at home plate could handle the network
of possible decisions: position yourself closer
to the bag, prepare for the pickoff, tag up,
throw to first, bases must be loaded
for a force-out at home, cover second
in a double play, third during a sacrifice bunt,
avoid errors, watch base runners leading off,
create a favorable frame for the umpire,
keep your mitt inside the strike zone,
bring your good stuff, a cutter keeps the ball
away from the sweet spot, keep your head
if the pitch is wild, watch for line drives,
and don't forget to look alive out there.

We only had to know our cut-off man.
Throw to him, he'll do the rest.
And pay attention, they said, because we chased
more butterflies than flyballs. While pitchers
picked off runners we picked dandelions.
Counted clouds instead of outs.
We couldn't help it. Our dads
drove ice trucks, worked third shift
at the packaging factory and slept all day,
picked us up every other weekend
and took us to the homes they rented
where we rented movies, ordered pizza,
and slept in beds surrounded by stacked boxes.

Yet somehow we still felt safe in their arms,
their arms that were tired. But still good.
We learned from our dads all we could
in the time we had, how to throw a fist,

drive a stick, pick up girls, catch a break.
Our coaches must have known all this.
That's why they hushed their sons
when we dropped the ball, were too scared to swing,
or forgot to slide when we stumbled into second.
That's why they let us see ourselves
in their sunglasses when, after the game
ended, they knelt down to us,
put their hands on our shoulders,
called us son and asked how things were at home.

# At the Golf Course After Hours

The dads who've cried here
I've hated, but I try to rake out grins for them
in the sand trap where I've been making snow angels.

While they sleep like holes, I stand on the ninth tee box
and try mouthing an apology to them in three strokes
or less. The only mouth I'll ever have is this one,
I know how it works, how it often fails, falls
short, hence its tendency to stay closed.

Just off the fairway, in the damp grass
thick enough to sound under my steps,
my apology sits wet with tears paternal,
having fallen. Forgot to keep my head down
like he told me, with his dry eyes.

I've one chance at this. If only I had someone
to hold my bag while I decide. My teeth throb.
See how well you'd finish this
with the trees and their shadows in the way.

Do you know your father? Teach me him,
his stance. Give me reason enough to please drop this
in the water and accept the loss.

# To Franz Wright

We met once in the space of a dream
no wider than a worm's mouth.
Your voice tree-rhythmic, you told me
something I've forgotten.

The winter light I'd call your voice
caught me early on, and I wilted.
Then I woke. In life I wrote you letters
that never fell on the right day.
That's okay.

You were the bearded skeleton
I feared as a child stayed
in the closet behind my church clothes
and waited for me
to leave my bed at night.

But at 21 on my knees at a bookstore
I found you again and your
"Moonlit winter clouds the color of the desperation of wolves."
then read every page, flipped through them
like I was searching for my favorite old shirt,
and you leapt out—into me
smelling of the dark I thought I'd left
in my wake, the dark
staring me down when I close my eyes.

I'll try to remember I write this
to the no one you might be now.

Or that compared to the vast language
of the eternal wind you wear
formally from one dream to another
this may resemble more the voice
of a timid child on stage
reciting lines she learned an hour ago.

Even so I can't help hoping,
when I see a bare branch
gesticulating against the blank page
of a cloudy afternoon,
the right day finally,
that it's you writing back

# Hump Day

And on the third day, in the desert still,
Jesus took up his needle and stabbed it through
the camel's eye, while in the kingdoms of the world
rich men were putting on their bright robes
and sitting down to breakfast, sure
of what was and was not possible.

## Sneeze

Thank you. I need
a blessing. April slowly
opening her eyes on the hillsides

breathes down warm to us
the kinds of perfumes Whitman
would, in his rooms, smell, and smile,

and cry, and trudge
to his desk for a pencil,
his scream to send

years-long toward us
into the soil we step through. But
I still feel no joy? I walked out

from dark hallways, hoping for some ease,
and found a nice breeze,
the birds' returning prayers, so why

do I feel in all of it such cruelty
today? Such rejection?
I tried to hold it in

so no one would notice, but you did
stepping from your car, and turning
toward a grove of trees. But I'm pleased

to have you as my priest
hearing this confession
and politely offering your pardon.

# To the Shroud of Turin

I'm careful, when facing someone,
not to knife with my eyes
the wrong part of their face, a mole, say,
whose prominence steers one easily away,

or the spruce of an eyebrow just long enough
to distract. It's like testing the ice
with your foot. So I wonder
what He must have pressed bloodily into you

that day, if you curled around His forehead,
staining you with his
and our filth he hadn't cast off
yet. And the rest

of him, to glove around the hands, of course,
a source of health and peace pierced
as they were, how cold were they before
they disappeared? I'm thirty-three

and haven't faced myself enough
to reckon with a fiber's worth of eternity,
or the buoyancy of suffering one sees
in the fabric of the clouds.

He must have whispered one secret into you,
one stratagem against some fact of life
still cloaked from us.
Those words printed on the page you are,

I'd read them and learn and maybe turn
away from my way of life.
Unless they're right, and you never held him
to begin with, to end with.

In which case, somewhere a thread of grace
must still lie in you. I'll press my face

against the glass, like a foot to the ice,
and hope. I don't know what I'd do otherwise.

# Taxonomy

I never learned the names of birds until today—
now everything sounds like the name of a bird.

This morning I preened a rare breed
of splinter from my heel,
then flipped through a flock of leaflets
on my desk so I could find the right insurance
because some shingles
had migrated from my roof
to the ground during a thunderstorm.

In the afternoon I spotted some rare
North American wood-rot roosting in my deck,
and pecked at it for an hour
with the beak of a wrench.

The stench was foul as I plucked up
the plumage of feces in my yard.

Then the haunting call of a heckler fell upon me
as he flew by in his Firebird.

At dinner, a flash of nausea washed over me
as I struggled to swallow
the remnants of a leftover mince-pie
that had been nesting at the back of my fridge.

I craned my neck a bit, the clouds warbled
and soon a gentle squall lit upon us,
filling the sky, putting the air on.

When the storm passed, I heard the birds
slowly return to the remaining daylight.

I listened without understanding,
without brooding on my ignorance,
instead clutching it to myself,

letting it rest in me a moment
so I could know it well enough
to fledge away from it when I was ready.

# Out of Order

I drop my quarters in before I notice
the sign. If order were in,
I'd ask it for more than pretzels.
I wonder, why does the fabric of my life
feel so twisted? I push
the change-return button that returns no change
then take my sandwich to the bench
by the river filling with fallen leaves.

As a kid, October was fruitful and sweet,
the nights were as long as nights.
Mom would open the cedar chest with a key
unfold my sweaters, hold them up
against me and say, *Still fits*.
She'd empty their pockets before
stacking them carefully in the drawers
where she always kept my sweaters
in colder months.

Warm enough today though to spend
an afternoon with the water
unraveling yesterday's downpour.
I swallow the last of my sandwich
and stand with a last look at the river.
I wonder how hard it would be to cross
today. Then I turn back
to the park entrance and start toward it
back to work, my left pocket, where I kept
my quarters, lighter now, and quieter.

III.

# Thumb War

Two students sitting across from each other
        hook the borders of their fingers together.

His advantage is strength and size but
        she knows he wants to touch her hand as long as possible.

He doesn't know she doesn't care
        when he captures and pins her down

in the trench between his knuckle and hers.
        Though she loses, she doesn't lose.

He says, *How about this Friday night?*
        *No, thanks*, she says so casually.

*Sorry,* she adds. He shakes a hand
        palm-up like a flag, *No, no, it's cool,*

he says trying not to look wounded.
        He places his hands on the counter

and coughs. *Maybe some other time?*
        *I don't know*, she says. Silence. The bell rings.

They lower their arms
        to grab their bags. She leaves slowly

like she's taking a tour.
        He leaves quickly, like he's taking fire.

# Love Poem

If I love every blemish on your skin
I'll remove the period at the end of a poem
and put it on my lips to give to your lips.

If I touch you the way winter touches a hill
you will feel flowers dying all over your body.

If the ceiling is full of sounds
my stomach is full of sounds.

If the priest hates you God loves you.
If we install enough windows in the ground
souls in hell will see forgiveness in the stars.

If ever you fill me with more emptiness
I'm whatever a grave is called
when only sunlight lies in it.

If your eye has a night inside it
it's always the first night, the night rewritten,
the night we spoke to each other like basements,
one crowded with silent wolves.

And if that night somehow brings us to the ocean
we'll be ourselves in it until we speak to each other
the way it speaks to itself. Until our selves are it.

Like the ocean I will be a question no one can answer.
Like the shore, you will be a sentence that never ends

# I'm in the Attic: a Dream-Memory

To Emily

I'm in the attic on a school night, opening windows
when I hear my own voice, a minute-long, leaf-like moan
spire down the sidewalk through an hour of trees
into the night. I follow. My hands are with me.
For now they speak for me, silent and drenched in shade.

The sidewalk became my favorite place
the night we met. I said nothing when we parted,
just plucked a bookmark from the nearest Bible
to plant between your lips so I'd remember where we left off.
I knew you'd guide me through a garden of fists.

Because of the flags descending silver
with autumn's silver light leftover, I know
I'm in the city still. Most of me. And my hands
in that light find their sound, leaf-like, but sad, because
the two of them alone can't cultivate applause.

I've lost my place. I've lost my voice. I remember
reading your body with my hands like a blind person.
What am I telling myself from a distance? What verses
for you burn unsung until I catch what I want to say?
Maybe what I want to say to *my* body is "Yes."

When I find my voice, I'll find you again.
And you'll remember my voice touching you
from the inside. You'll remember that, when we came
together, we left the window open, our voices overlapping,
and the trees, for an hour in the wind, were clapping.

# Before Cursing God, I Pray to My Wife

I've forced you to sleep too many nights alone
beside me. I've let you cry
in a room you'd built for us
while I built my life into a cell
and made you the window I look out of.

But I tell you the silence in me
would miss your voice.
The first week I ever spent without you was you
creating my world in seven days. I tell you

happy people bother me, but happy
is still what I hope you are
because if I'd never met you
I'd never have met me.

This little life we've made
is bigger than any word. Any wound
I've convinced myself has its own shores.

I say little the way most might say,
"Jupiter, from here, seems little." The way
someone says, "A little," after someone asks,
"Are you afraid of dying?"

I wish I could think of a better word for our life,
but I've never seen a star up close.
I've never swallowed a garden
and felt a thousand species living and dying inside me.

I've only sat in the corner at a wedding recently
and watched you dance
through three songs without me. Three.

Which is how many times the word happy
happens in this poem,
it's how many people in one

God is, they say, and it's how many times
I've had to learn to live without you.

Three is enough. Even for God apparently.
So after the third song,
I stood up in that crowded reception hall,
and went out to meet you.

# A Pond Walk

After James Schuyler

Can I tempt you to a pond walk?
Can I hold you like a priest holds an urn?
And can we lie somewhere off the path
in the spindles of timothy and goldenrod?

Behind every cloud is another cloud,
said Judy Garland. One sentence
hides another and is another as well,
wrote Kenneth Koch. So here's

my little vial of liquid paper
my puddle of silence and sky
should I need to hide a sentence
under another, which happens

often. If you only knew what words
reach out for you under the hedgerow
and how laden with rocks
the soil of my fear that holds

in place this pale forsythia
I planted last March in case,
when asked to the pond, you
putting down your book said, well, yes.

# A Bridge of Paper

To walk across a bridge of paper,
she says, is to know my thoughts at night.
Then she pops an antacid, turns over
and tries to sleep. The house is finally quiet,
the cat put away in the basement.
I sit at my desk with a piece of paper.
I write, *To walk across a bridge of paper,*
then stare for a while, sipping my coffee.
She scribbles herself between our sheets.

All she wants, I think is to feel blank,
not always, but for a few hours a day at least,
to know the direction of the current
under our feet as we cross, because if she wanted
she could write a book in her sleep.
I'm realizing her admission was an invitation.
She doesn't need an editor, just a reader.

I come back to bed and switch off
the light, erasing the room for now.
We'll talk about it tomorrow.
*She'll talk*. I'll cook her some eggs,
or maybe just some toast, something to bite
between words, something over which
to spread her sentences. I'll dot them
with little affirmations. *Uh huh, I see,
Go on, I'm sorry*, carefully making room
for the next step if it comes. And if it doesn't,
we'll wait together for the house to quiet
down again, for the day to turn over,
and hopefully for the whispering
pages make against each other.

## Diagnosis

At the doctor's office,
what her hand did to my hand
was like lips thirsting past
the lip of a cup.
And *her* lips, what they did
that night to my neck
was like a cut flower
swelling against its price tag,
celebrating the time it has left
in its temporary vessel.

What my voice does to her name
this morning, Sunday,
waking her early,
is like a choir before mass practicing
to an empty church,
the belfry of her arms
silent above her head.

Then what she does
when she turns over
and drifts back to sleep,
it is like a leaf
wanting back the ground
that grinds the tree upward
at a dream's pace.

Which of us will be alone?
No need to wonder for now, but
what would I compare to
the crease in the sheet
where her body should be?

*Nothing*, the doctor had said.
*I'd call it abnormal, at most.*
*But temporary.*
What isn't? I thought.

What doesn't
share a sense of ending
while not wanting to?

Anyway, *this*. This
feeling of wanting nothing,
sitting on the porch
letting her sleep,
short as it may be,
and the hush it makes
washing over me,
under me, it's maybe like
the sound an answer
to a prayer makes pushing past,

which is also like the silent strafe
of that bird blurring
between our heads
while we walked
at the park one day last week.

It passed so swiftly
and unseen, we stopped
she and I
and turned around
to see what we heard
like two strangers
with the same name called
from the back of the room.

# Imagining Us in a Jewelry Commercial

If I biked us down a city street,
you on the handlebars in a skirt
and high-heeled sandals, I'd keep control
no more than three feet before
I hit a curb and you fell to the pavement,
maybe scraping a knee. Then you'd stand
and walk home without a word
while I followed, dragging the bike in silence.

And suppose we drove a convertible
through winding mountain passes.
*Would* you stand and put your arms up,
smiling as your fingers weaved
through folds of clean night air? Or
would we not put up the top to keep the cold
out? Would you not drive since you
otherwise feel sick through such precarious turns?

If you came home to find the house dark,
a candle and box on the table with a note
that read, "Turn around." you'd no doubt
be surprised to find me behind you,
so surprised you'd shudder, say, "God!" and "sorry,"
while I turned on the lights, apologizing too,
then I'd wipe down the counter, cook some rice
and ask you about your day.

On the off chance we'd attend an affluent ball,
I wouldn't follow you through the halls
while you seductively turned a bare shoulder
to gaze back at me. No. We'd both
be busy wondering why the hosts had hired
dancers in silver skintight jumpsuits
unfolding a routine involving firey batons,
ribbons, and giant steel rings.

In fact, we'd likely leave early, and by the time

the silk curtain peeled back to reveal
the pendant I'd never buy you because
you wouldn't want me to spend "that kind of money"
on something you'd never wear, we'd already
be settled into bed where'd I'd pick
an old movie, and you'd fall asleep after pulling me
closer, laughing, asking me to keep you warm.

## We Must Go

I'm usually happy when my kids are happy.
My daughter chases a bubble across the yard.
My son digs a hole in the sand with a stick.

Leaves click their tongues like fire as a breeze ribbons
from the west and lands cold in the grass.
They don't mind. They're having fun, aren't they.

But I know soon I'll tell them it's getting dark
and we need to go, and life
will have turned against them.

And I, on behalf of life, will say I'm sorry
as I buckle seatbelts
against their will, against their cries for mercy.

I'll lie. Maybe tomorrow, I'll say.
I'll do this to move them forward
because tomorrow won't be like today. There will be

appointments, errands, a drifting from place to place.
In the morning, my wife and I will gather them
from their beds and bring them with us

where we must go. But for now
let her try to catch that bubble
before it bursts. Let him see how far down

the hole goes. Why not?
It's not dark yet,
and there's nowhere we have to be.

# My Children Sleeping

They lie like two doors
from a church burned down. No,
they lie like rain in a stranger's hand.
And I look at them
like a rose looks at two thorn-sized cuts
in someone's thumb. No,
I look at them like a river
looks at either of its banks as it passes
and approaches them at the same time.
And like a river feeling the syllable
of every one of its stones,
I feel what I've said to them all day
aging already inside me. No,
inside *them*. I want to reach
for those words, wrench them out.
No, I think, you'll wake them.

I'm reminded of the day,
when I was nine, I reached
for two robin's eggs
nesting in our front yard's crabapple tree.
*Don't touch them*, my mom had said.
They lay so blue, so
burdened with the burning
foretaste of flight,
I thought I'd be touching
the doors to the sky but, *No*,
she said, *if you disturb the shell,*
*you risk killing the life inside.*

## In the Gray Yard

In what my son calls the gray yard,
he and I walk between headstones
while he counts birds and subtracts them

from fake flowers.
I'm subtracting death years
from birth years.

He was 73, she 88. Another
35, beloved husband and father.
The arithmetic matters. Numbers

are black and white.
Real asters lift their heads near fences
for no other reason save it's May.

My son knows he can't count those.
Overcast without rain today,
sky the color of smoke, a vale

between the sun and us as we walk
until I feel a drop drop cold
on my forehead, then one in my eye

when I look up. We should go,
I say. But he wants to stay.
Well, I don't control the weather.

Honestly, I don't know if the rain
will fall any harder than this
but it's cold and I want to get back

to the smell of woodsmoke and old books,
back to our life parked almost
a block from here, here where the peace

is overwhelming. At our house

I like how thin the windows are
and how they rattle when cars pass.

I like the kitchen light in the evening
and the way Emily has arranged
the furniture in the living room.

But I don't like the back door
that doesn't shut completely
or the toilet that still leaks. I don't like

how close the sidewalk is
to our front door, or how cold
the patio gets in winter.

Here, it's so quiet, I can hear the grass move,
and I like that, and I don't like that.
Same for the cracked pavement

weaving between the rows
and the sound of a dog
somewhere far off fighting its chain.

I tell him again we have to go,
which he doesn't like,
but I count, for him, what he likes:

his trains, his Legos, his crayons
all waiting for him at home.
This is enough to turn him around

at least. What gets him
moving is my promise
that someday we'll come back.

# Walking on the Beach with My Son

He asks if we're going to die.
I say yes this time. At first
he says nothing. Then he says
he and I are parents to each other.
He looks at the water and says
he can make a better ocean in his room.

He doesn't know he builds
a separate ocean
in me when he's in pain
or that my arms held my mother
to practice holding him.
I kneel to him, we keep each other close.

We're like people made of water.
Anyone who's died
may drink or swim in us
and know the quiet hurt
stars teach us if we forget
ourselves enough to listen.

# Lost

At three-years-old, he dropped
a crayon down the air vent
straight through the floor into the crevices of the house
where it probably settled into some
unreachable space between the basement wall
and the foundation. But as far as
he was concerned, it had fallen
into colorlessness, and through the ceiling
I could hear how he mourned it.

When he finally calmed himself enough
to tell me what had happened,
I tried to let him know that there were
in excess of probably a million
other crayons in the world just like it,
just as red, wrapped in the same strip
of off-red paper, having the same smooth surface,
the same acrylic smell,
that there would likely be millions,
maybe billions, more molded, packaged,
and shipped out in the coming years,
and that, in fact, in that instant,
two more red crayons of his own
rested contentedly in the little box
he kept under his bed. Perfectly safe.

But none of that helped because he wasn't thinking
about pictures of fire trucks
settling for an unorthodox blue paint-job
or autumn scenes with an abundance
of only yellow and orange.
His concern was that *that* red crayon was gone.
And he was responsible.

I tried taking him outside to cheer him up,
showing him how pretty the sunset was
but the deep blush of the horizon only reminded him

and he broke down again.
He squeezed his red eyes shut
and buried his red face in my shirt.
And since it was all I could do,
I carried him into the kitchen
and fixed him a pancake
and poured him a glass of milk,
because he was suddenly hungry,
before I gave him a bath and cleaned his face
and put him to bed,
leaving his door open just enough
to let the light come in.

# Most People Think the Sky

*I want to kill heaven
with an axe,*
my son said in the garden
for the rabbit we'd buried there
the day after a letter came
for the man who'd died
in our kitchen
before we moved in.

*Then no one will have to go,*
he said and asked where heaven was.
Had I known
I'd have told him
maybe. Instead
I entered again the garden
that evening
after putting the kids to bed
then grabbed the shovel and put it,
and hopefully the whole matter,
in the garage, where
I keep my axe and my ladder.

# Grandma's Kitchen

This is the place poetry professors obsess over.
They hand you a pencil and say
*Show me something honest and painful.*
The problem is I can't find the pain
that isn't there in Grandma's kitchen. I'd sit
under her table with a book
on tape, the kind that began
*Whenever it's time to turn the page
you'll hear the chimes ring like this:*

I'd sit there, in a self-inflicted cage
listening to the story, hearing her beyond,
clacking dishes from the sink, shaking
her vial of zinc she took every night.
Occasionally lighting a cigarette.
The alarm on her dryer yawned
louder than Grandpa a room away in his chair.

I'm trying, Professor. Somewhere
something devastating must be stirring under
the soapy surface of this scene.
But Grandma hums her hymn
so carelessly she can't be lonely.
You should see her slight grin
and the stack of dishes, cartoonishly tall.

But, Professor, I remember now
from time to time she *would* still her body
and sigh. I'd ask *What's wrong?* No answer.
I'd think, *Must be the ringing in her ears.*
No one knew it was the sound of cancer.

She tried describing it to me once,
the ringing. *Constant, like the highest key
on a church organ, like a cage made of voice.
You don't know if you're the only one
hearing it—which can be lonely.* Then she spread

a layer of flour on the counter
and rolled out a lump of dough
to pound. The weight
of the room would lift a bit. Then I had to wait
for her to bake it into bread, so
she could cut and serve it to me
first, one last time, her way of professing
my importance, as if I didn't know.

# Remembering How She Died

What I forget is the wind
when Grandma closed her mouth. Did it shift
like a sheet through fingers of winter trees?
Or let itself down and pause
with the frost,
slowly sharpening the grass's edges?

What I forget is the window. Closed.
Had I seen a blank page of snow
spread on the ground waiting for spring
to write us in ink the color of damp dirt,
inviting us to dig and bury seeds
for vegetables we'd eat that summer, their muscle
seasoned with breezes from an open window?

And the falling
maybe it's slower than standing still.

She remembered me
almost a minute, long enough
to ask about my newborn son, long enough
to laugh through the closing curtains of her chest
and in that minute, I was hers again.

Ten-years-old, I sat at her coffee table
with her markers, drawing trees
in her notebook she'd picked up
at a Rotary meeting. She hung the tree
on her fridge, and smiled
back to the spaghetti.

The minute ended. Wind
may have slowed westward
toward sunset on the highway I'd take home.
She may have opened her eyes once more
in a panic. With a morphine drip that strong,
the nurse said, the feeling of falling

so overwhelms the mind, one startles awake
and remembers her whole life in an instant
before floating back up to the cloud
her mind has become.

# IV.

VI

# A Box

I nailed myself inside the box
so I could hide from the other boxes.
Jill came by. She needed help with the latest figures.

At the time, it was cold inside the box
and the fleas bit while performing quadrilles
across my forehead. I could hear Jill getting her crowbar
again. Life in the box was simpler. I had time
to think, to walk and admire
the stars as they shifted in and out
behind a thin sheet of blue cloud delicate
as the innocent love you have for others
and of which they're not aware.

I found a new way to use language
inside the box.
Thoughts came easily, and the words for them,
new words for light, new words for salvation,
for patriotism. In the language they spoke
inside the box, the word for death and the word for life
were the same word. I visited the new school
they'd built inside the box, but it looked
like an old one, maybe because the word for old
and the word for new were the same
in the language they spoke
inside the box.

The students mostly sat in the halls with their violins,
the ones given to them by their fathers,
who'd all died in the terrible war that had greatly shaped
how people lived inside the box,
though many years had passed since then,
so most of us weren't aware of it anymore,

which was the point. The word for war
and the word for home were the same word
inside the box.

The students all played different melodies.
At least it seemed that way at first,
but I stood still a long time
until the different melodies flowed together
in a fugue that reminded me of something I'd heard
in my youth outside the box. I don't think
the word for harmony and the word for harmony
are the same word inside the box.

It was during my third year inside the box
I met Nancy, who had kind eyes,
a steady job in healthcare, a booming industry
inside the box. And she listened. "Tell me
about your fear of boxes," she would say.
And you could tell she wasn't just making small talk.
We walked on the beach together. We kissed.
We found a hotel and made love for the first time.
Only a month later, we married on that same beach
inside the box. After our son and daughter were born,

Nance and I saw each other more than we talked.
The kids grew. Nancy one day said, "I hate you!" I said,
"I hate you too!" The word for hate and the word for love
are not the same word inside the box,
but they sound pretty similar.
The kids lived with her. Then they lived with me
inside the box. Our broken war. I mean home.

One day I was walking by the new ancient ruins
inside the box when a strong pain in my back
brought me to the ground.
The doctors used a lot of words like "malignant" and "spreading."
I told myself these words might mean something else
inside the box.

Nancy sat by the bed.
I told her I was sorry. Inside the box

the word for sorry and the word for human are the same word.
She kissed me and said, "I love you. I never stopped."
"I hate you too," I said, because I was having trouble speaking.
Then I felt something crawling on my forehead.
I felt cold. Then came a great crashing sound, a rush

of fluorescent light, an electric humming.
Through the hole, Jill looked down at me
with trepidation. "I need your help," she said.
"These numbers aren't right, and the boss
is literally breathing down my neck."
"Jill," I said, "we've been over this. That's not how you use
the word literally." "No, look," she said. I squinted.
Behind her was a dark figure
bending down toward the back of Jill's neck.

## The Balloon

from our son's first birthday
the week before, the one that,
as it deflated a breath of helium
every few hours, bobbed
across the ceiling
rattling like a garbage bag,
its string tangling in the ceiling fan.

When one of the spinning blades
struck the flimsy imitation-foil
with a horrid crash, we both sat up in bed,
and you said, "What was that?"
before the fan began striking it over and over
and the downstairs filled with a constant thrashing
we knew was someone
turning over furniture, opening doors. You lifted
our son from his bassinet beside us
and held him as I locked
the door to our room and called 911.
The operator stayed on
until the patrolman arrived and let himself in.
He called us down—
by then the fan had lashed the paper open—
he was shining his light to it, trying
to suppress a smirk
while he chewed his gum.

I looked at its shredded body hanging
like the flag of a fallen nation
and shook my head and exhaled
remembering your eyes upstairs
as I'd held your face to mine
and told you we would be okay, don't worry,
though deep down
I was sure our lives were over.

# Hotel Room

Give me four walls
papered in vinyl paisley
and bedecked in framed prints
of imagined places, or quotes
about what constitutes the "good life"
so I can rest in forgotten allowances
of my lost adolescence.
Let my worn clothes
lie crumpled on the pale carpet
beside candy wrappers
and empty soda cans. Let my bed
unmade remain silent.

Someday I will kill this boy in me
and finally sleep, and stop
waking in the middle of the night
afraid of some strange presence
unseen and remember
at home two children who know
me as Dad. I'll prefer
a detached and pleasant existence,
walk in the park by the river at twilight,
drink coffee by an open window.

In the kitchen, I'll turn the music up
to drown the outside noise
while chopping vegetables
my first night back. I'll look up
a moment to smile
at you reading at the table
who'll be sharing with me
the comfortable allowances
of what we'll call "the good life."

# I'm Still Finding Dead Marigolds

on the floor where my daughter leaves them.
They're older than me, she says,
so I have to kill them.

They turn to paper in the corners of rooms,
gathered like garbage,
graying like the wrong clouds.

They whisper back when I drowsily kick them
late hours on my way to the bathroom.
I usually apologize. Why?

Today she abducts another from the flower bed
and leaves it on the porch
for the storm this evening.

If the wind tries hard enough tonight
it'll gather petals up and add
a bit more gold to her October air

that pencils with rain the stains of old leaves
on the new sidewalk. For now
I don't know when I'll deal with the dust

on the floor. Some of it was us,
some debris of petal, stem, and blossom.

For now it's a familiar quiet
I thank for its honesty
before I sweep it away.

# Rain

Rain just before leaving the house.
Rain without thunder. Rain with thunder
that turns out to be someone
in the next room moving heavy furniture.
Rain enough to cancel games, moods, intentions.
Rain song and wren song stirring
in the branches, cancelling the voices of leaves.
Rain slowing down on sidewalks
and branching into the curves of roads,
draining like false words into curb gutters.
Rain falling windward from clouds
the color and shape of whales, the color
and shape of waves frozen in mid-break.
Clouds quickly washing by, cringing east.
Rain on glass, on steel, on shadows and ashes.
Rain sliding through smoke and diminishing fire.
Rain in the veins of plants, powering plants
and animals, the grace of rain
and the veil of it blotting your view
of the fields in the evening.
Rain for one day and one night.
Rain on lips and eyebrows, on shoulders.
Rain changing your hair the rest of the day.
Rain sounding its squeeze in the cheeks of the soil
even after the rain stops, the sun comes out
again, and the smell of rain stays in the pavement.
Rain leaves eventually, fades out,
leaves cars and yards both rinsed and sullied,
leaves an eye of wet on the knee
should you bend down afterward in the grass
to pluck up a key half sunk in the sand
revealed by the rain, the rain rolling off
doors as they open
and neighbors saturate the atmosphere
with the sounds of their conversations.

# Eggs

*Up late with my father before he left for his tour of duty in Iraq*

It might've been raining.
The TV's blue glow
stirred nearly green with the kitchen-light.

Suddenly hungry, we found in his fridge
a slice of ham  I cut in half
and two eggs. The last two.

*You know how to cook eggs?* he asked.
I nodded, cracking the second,
separating it with one hand,

letting the yolk break, the albumen
stir into it and, as it cooked,
lose its transparency.

In the ghost show we watched,
two men in night vision walked
through unlit hallways whispering to themselves.

Having heard a knock
one of them suddenly stopped
and asked the ceiling, *Was that you?*

We heard the rain on the roof, I've decided
because when the weather is bad
there's time to interpret the white

space between two people, measure it
against others, see what hatches, and conclude
its texture as either good or bad.

*It's good*, he said
after taking his first bite.
*From now on you're makin' the eggs.*

# High Light

I took my yellow marker to the cemetery
because I have a horrible memory,
except the sunlight lit the names up for me,
so many, in fact, I forgot *my* name
and asked everyone who I was,
pressing my ear to the grass.

I said, Please raise your hand
if you're nothing but ashes.
And several winds that felt like arms lifted.
I remembered who I was again
and wrote my name on my hand in yellow.

I said to the sun, I wish my tongue
were made of mirror so everyone could see you
and themselves in every word I spoke.
I wish I could say to those I love,
I've written your name on the cave inside my skull,
drawn lines around it depicting movement,
and put my hand print on it
so I'll be touching it thousands of years from now.

I found a white bird crouching near a sepulcher
and colored its wings yellow
so it wouldn't forget how to fly.
I found a yellow flower
and made it more yellow
so it wouldn't forget to come back as itself in spring.
And I yellowed the dead grass
so it wouldn't forget it wasn't green.
And the fence around the cemetery
so we wouldn't forget borders don't keep us alive.
And the soles of my feet
so I'd make yellow tracks wherever
I walked and never forget where I'd been.
And my teeth so I could forget
how smiles are supposed to look.

And my eyelids so they wouldn't forget
to open again whenever they closed.

Then the sky yellowed itself because it was evening
and I'd lost track of time.
At night when I got home.
I didn't have my yellow marker anymore.
I'd thrown it as far as I could
toward the eastern horizon
so the sun wouldn't forget where tomorrow begins.

# How to Draw Fire

With your son's hand
small on your hand
guiding, warming it.

With a red crayon flickering toward
a center, pencil for smoke
rising hair-shaped on the page.

Windows early darkened by winter
staring like snuffed televisions.
The only light in the room
breathing louder than you.

And neighbors who night-walk past
seeing the light inside and you two
clearly conjuring spirits. And spirits

in the room believing
themselves clearly alive again,
because this warmth,

it must mean their blood
is trying to find once more
where their bodies begin.

# Afterlife

*After Ko Un*

I won't come back as a human.
I'll come back as an autumn mayfly
and live no more than a day. I'll remember
the leaf detaching, how much

my life had changed
by the time it landed in the pond,
how my wings expanded
faster than the rings the leaf made in the water.

Or maybe I'll come back as the water
or at least a fish who thinks
he's the water. Or maybe
I *will* come back as a human,

a human just like me. Maybe I have
already, several times, which is why
when I see someone I don't know
standing on a corner in the wind,

there's always something about them
reminds me of music I've only heard
inside myself those rare moments I forget
I once (or more than once) was born.

**Marcus Whalbring** grew up in southern Indiana. He lives there still with his wife and children where he works as a teacher. As an undergrad he began to write poetry with the encouragement of his teachers and continued to do so long after graduating. About a decade later he entered Miami University where he earned his MFA. He published his first book of poems in 2013. His work has appeared in *The Cortland Review, Spry, Underwood Press* and others

www.ingramcontent.com/pod-product-compliance
Lightning Source LLC
Chambersburg PA
CBHW070550090426
42735CB00013B/3140